It's Easy To Play Popular Classics.

Wise Publications
London / New York / Paris / Sydney / Copenhagen / Madrid

Exclusive Distributors:

Music Sales Limited
8/9 Frith Street, London W1V 5TZ, England.

Music Sales Pty Limited
120 Rothschild Avenue, Rosebery, NSW 2018, Australia.

Music Sales Corporation
257 Park Avenue South, New York, NY10010, United States of America.

Order No. AM952490
ISBN 0-7119-7166-8
This book © Copyright 1998 by Wise Publications.

Book design by Michael Bell Design.
Cover illustration by Nicky Dupays.
Compiled by Peter Evans.
Music arranged by Stephen Duro.
Music processed by Allegro Reproductions.

Your Guarantee of Quality:
As publishers, we strive to produce every book to the highest commercial standards.
The music has been freshly engraved and the book has been carefully designed to minimise awkward page turns and to make playing from it a real pleasure.
Particular care has been given to specifying acid-free, neutral-sized paper made from pulps which have not been elemental chlorine bleached.
This pulp is from farmed sustainable forests and was produced with special regard for the environment.
Throughout, the printing and binding have been planned to ensure a sturdy, attractive publication which should give years of enjoyment.
If your copy fails to meet our high standards, please inform us and we will gladly replace it.

Rondo in D minor

From "Abdelazer"

Music by Henry Purcell

Moderately

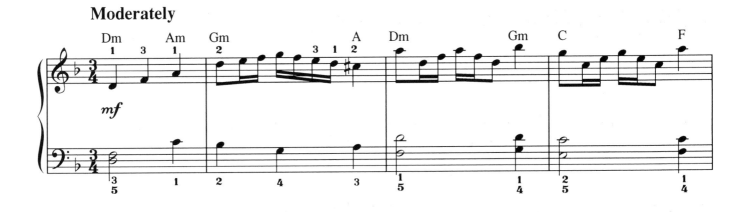

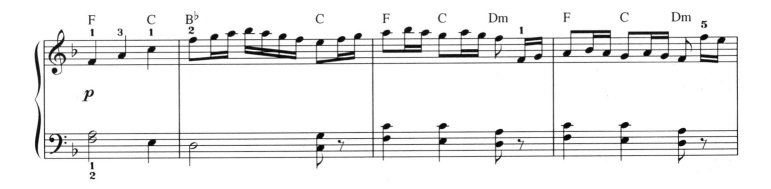

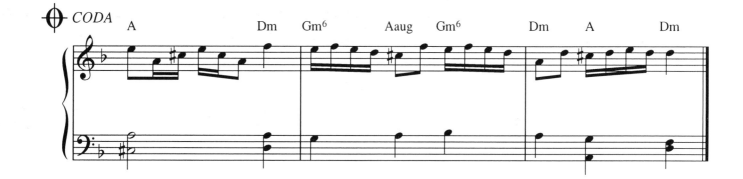

Larghetto
From Concerto Grosso No.12

Music by George Frideric Handel

Moderately

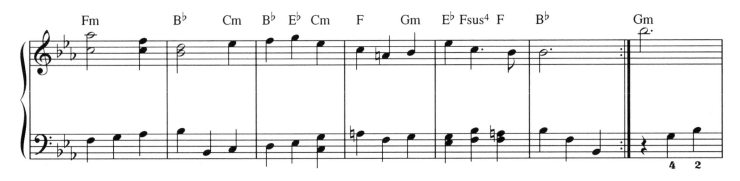

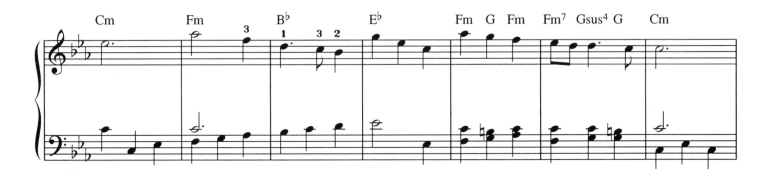

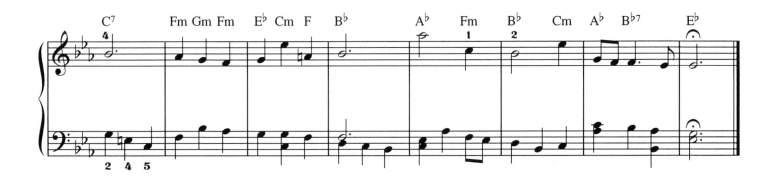

Theme

From String Quartet Op.3, No.5

Music by Joseph Haydn

Moderately

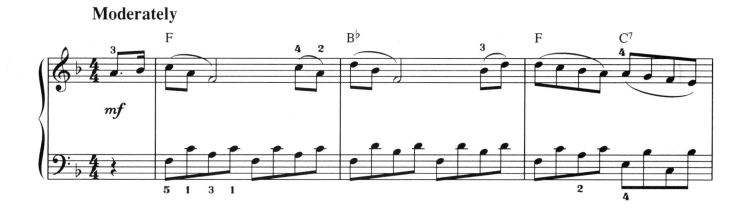

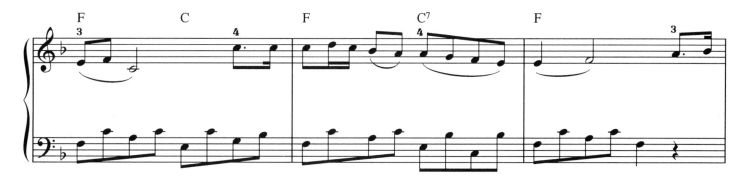

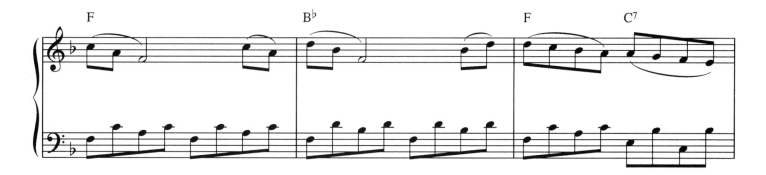

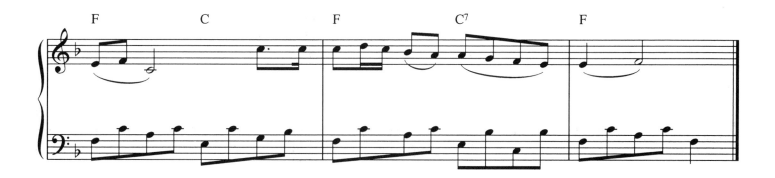

March

From the opera "Scipione"

Music by George Frideric Handel

With movement

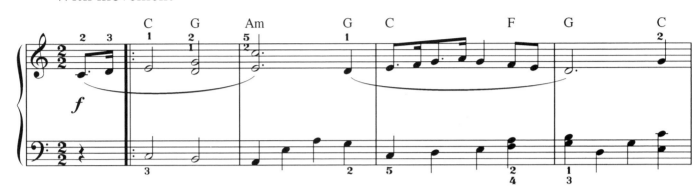

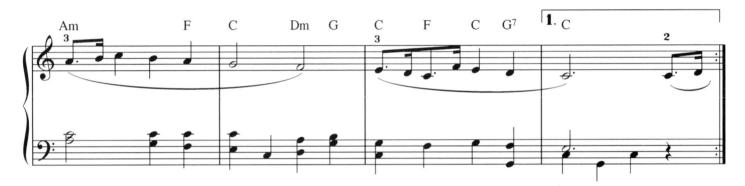

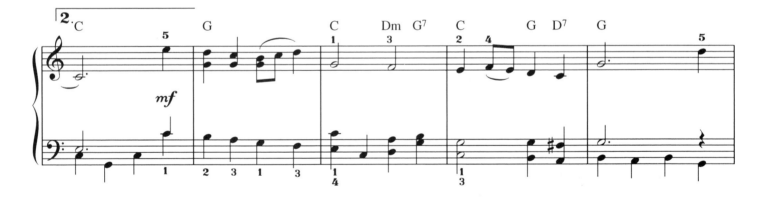

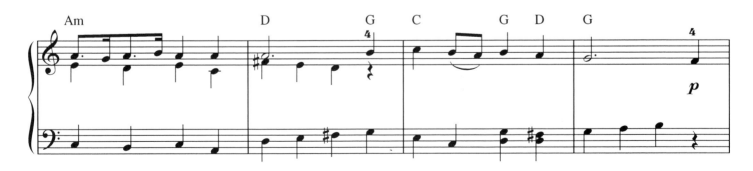

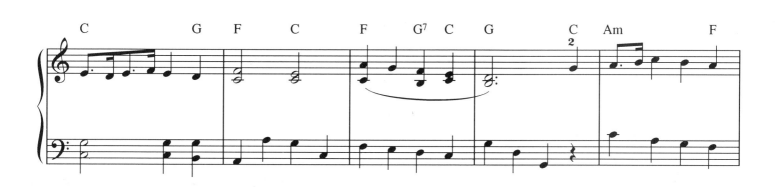

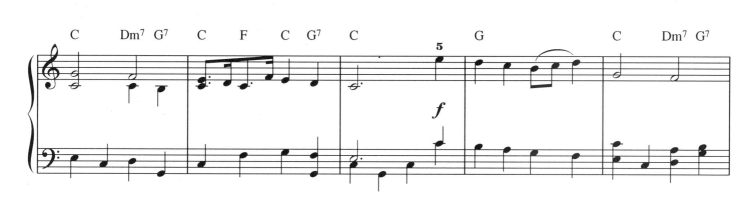

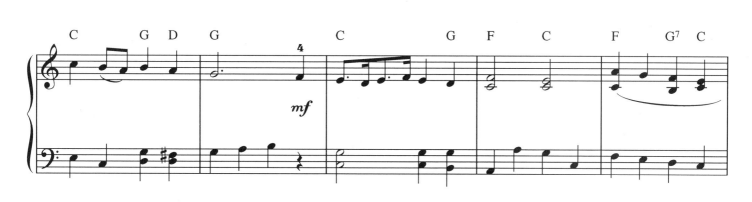

Air On The 'G' String

Music by Johann Sebastian Bach

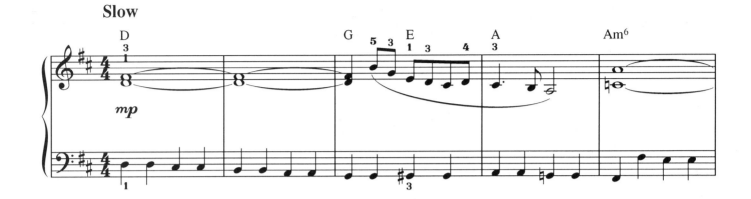

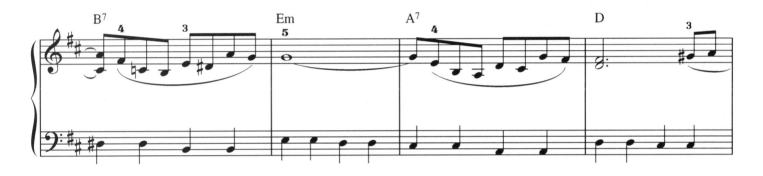

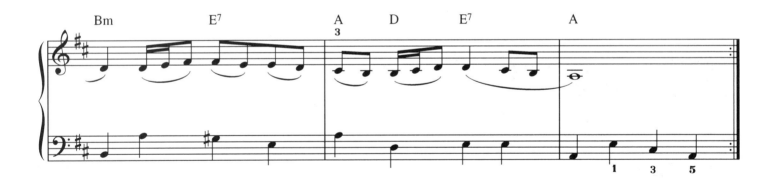

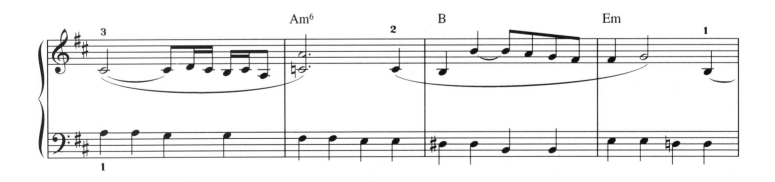

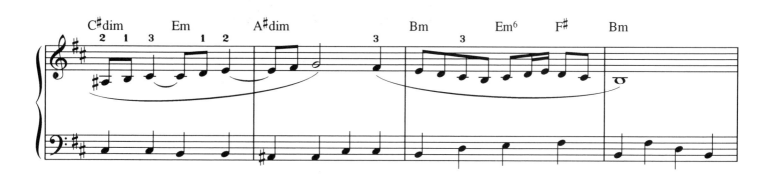

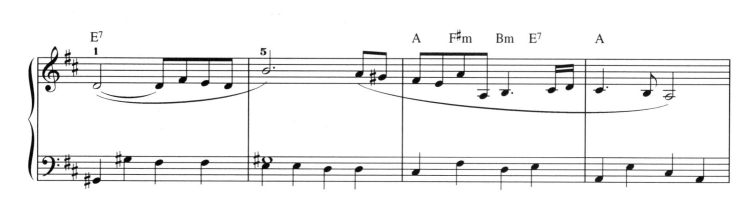

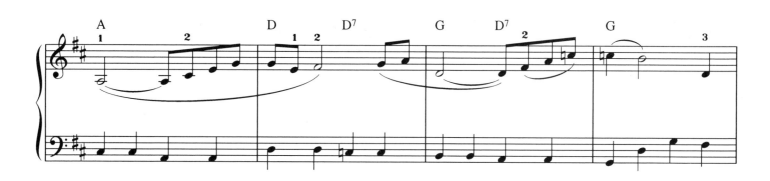

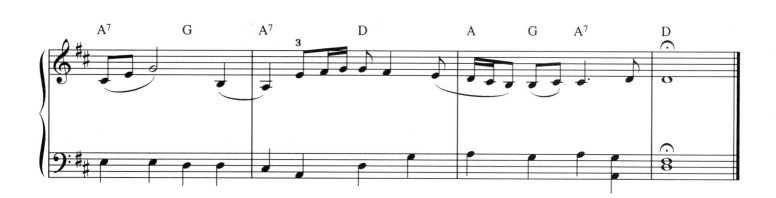

Tell Me Fair Ladies

From the opera "The Marriage Of Figaro"

Music by Wolfgang Amadeus Mozart

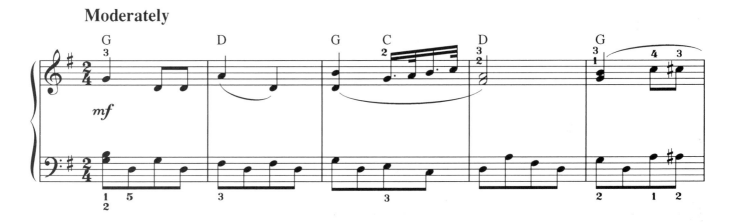

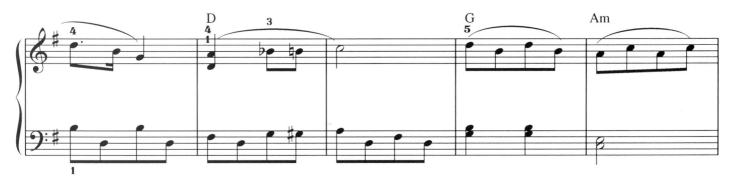

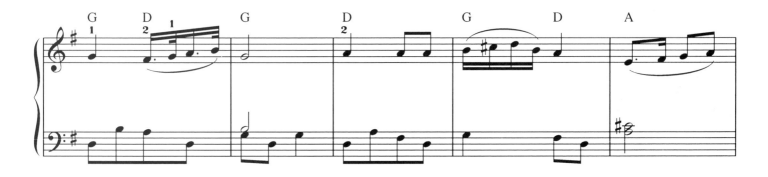

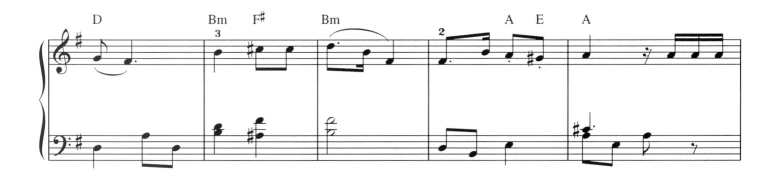

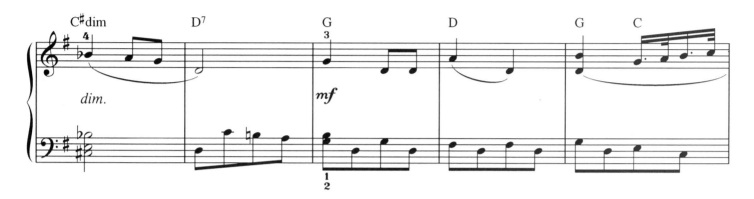

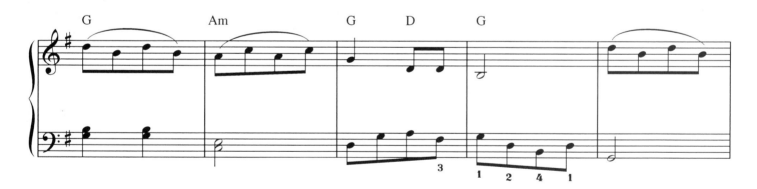

Theme

From Clarinet Concerto (2nd Movement)

Music by Wolfgang Amadeus Mozart

Moderately slow

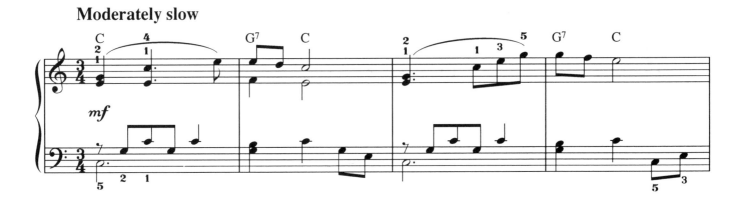

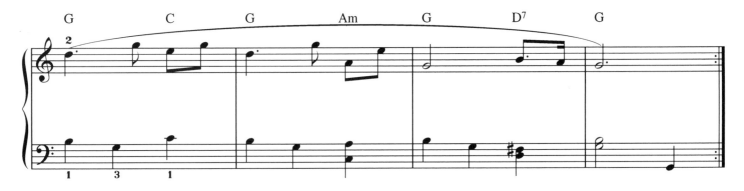

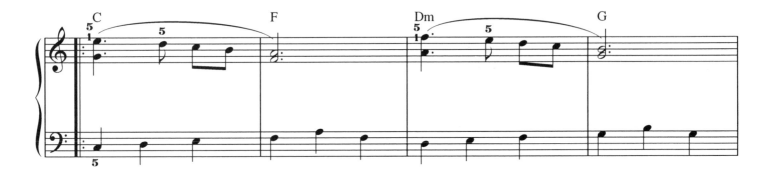

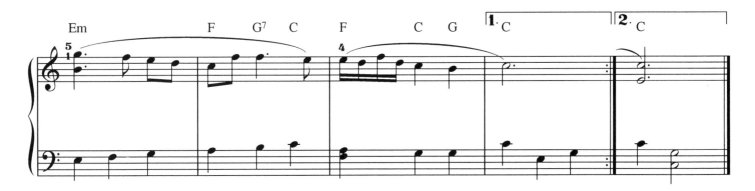

Ode To Joy

Music by Ludwig van Beethoven

With movement

Theme

From "Sonata Pathétique" (2nd Movement)

Music by Ludwig van Beethoven

Moderately slow

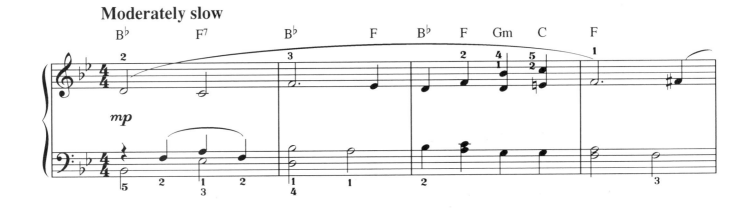

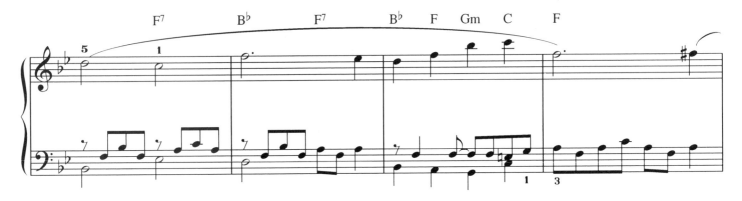

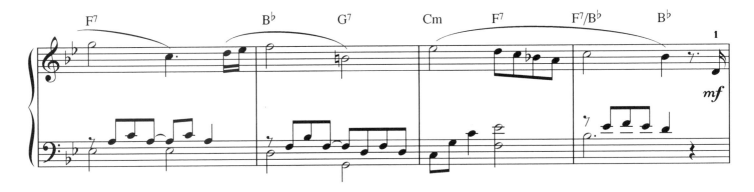

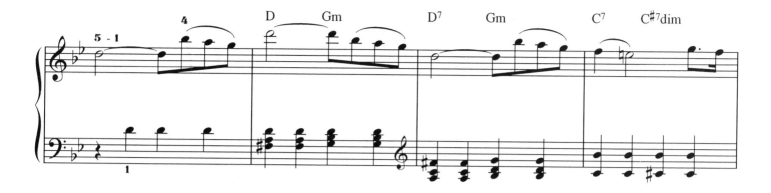

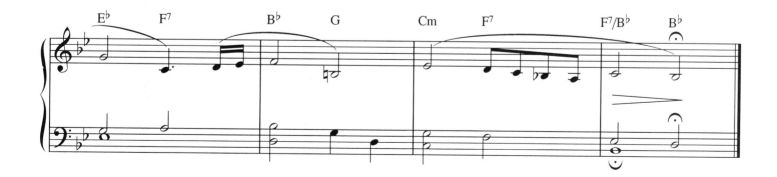

Minuet in G

Music by Ludwig van Beethoven

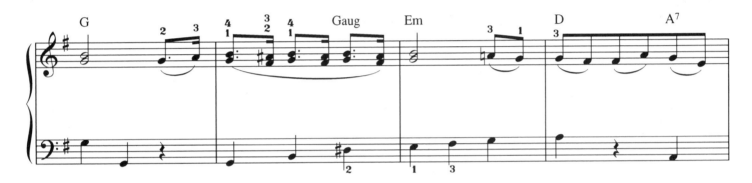

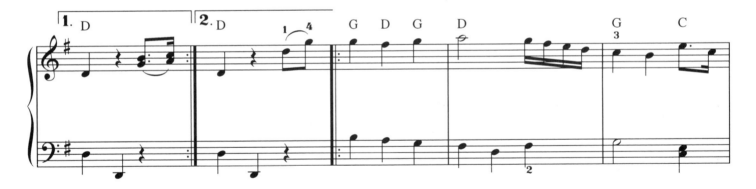

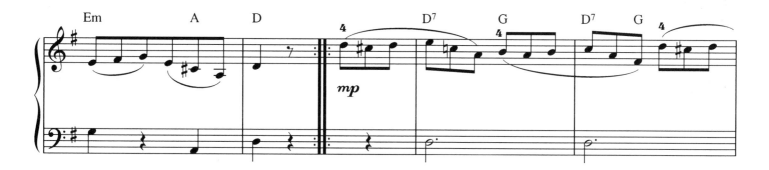

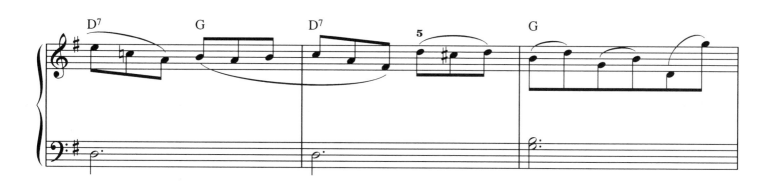

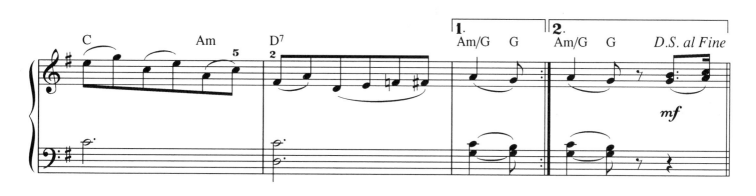

Für Elise

Music by Ludwig van Beethoven

Moderately

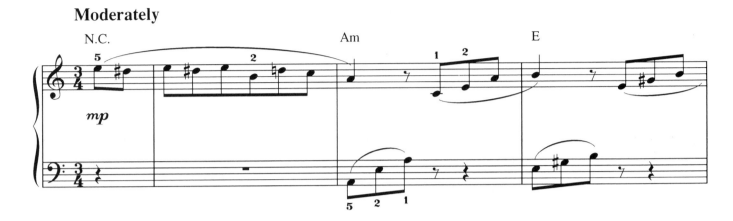

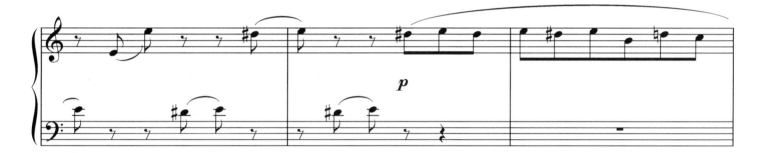

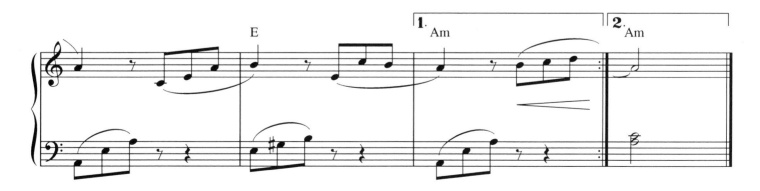

Ave Maria

Music by Franz Schubert

Moderately slow

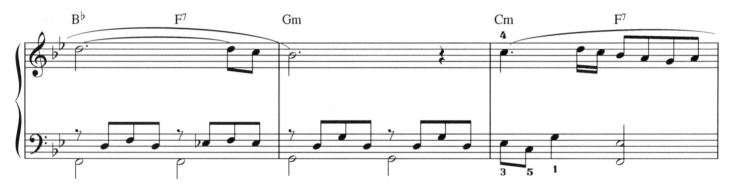

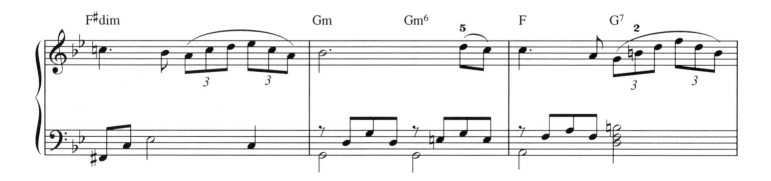

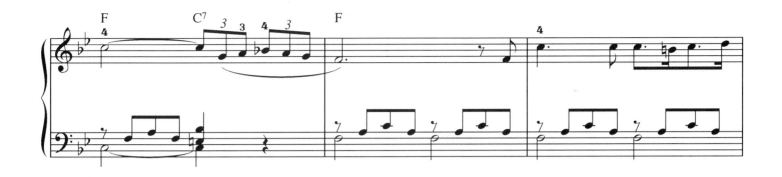

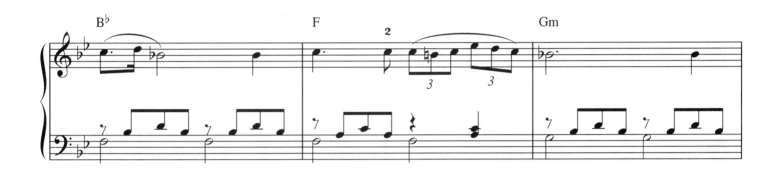

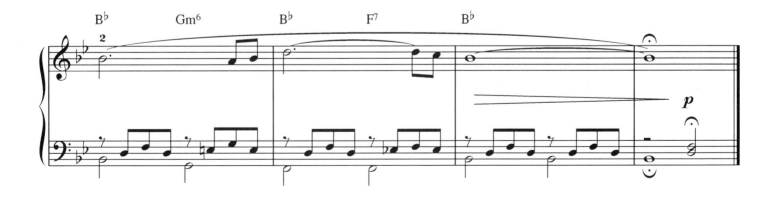

Theme
From Symphony No. 3 in F (2nd Movement)

Music by Johannes Brahms

Moderately

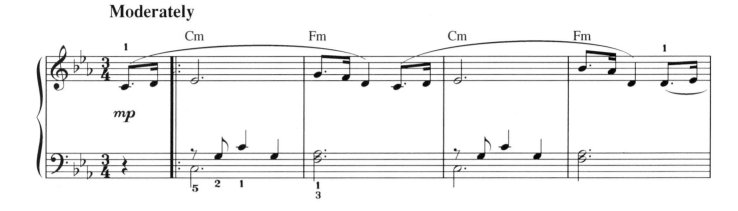

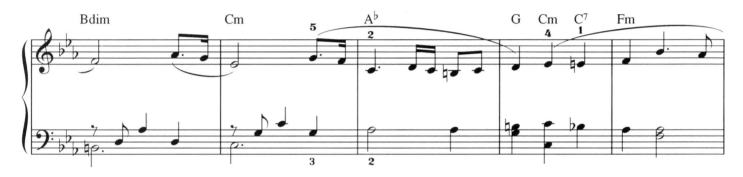

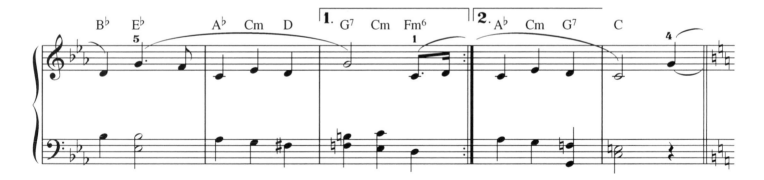

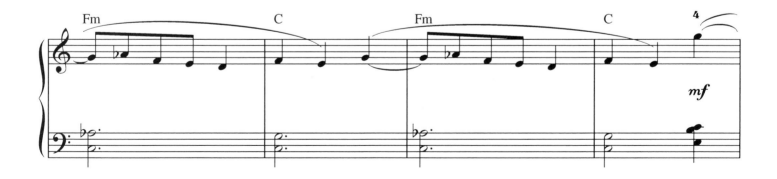

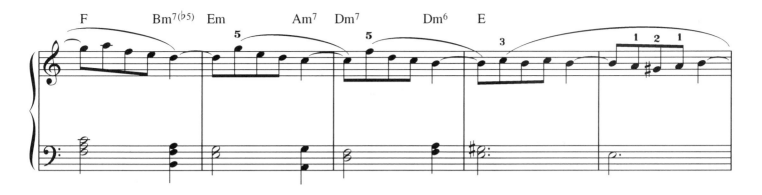

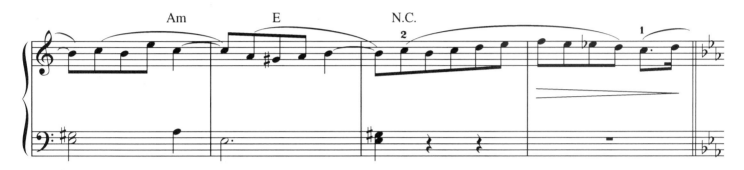

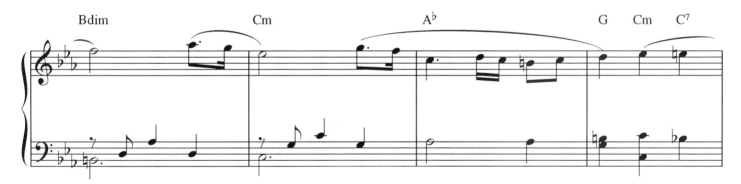

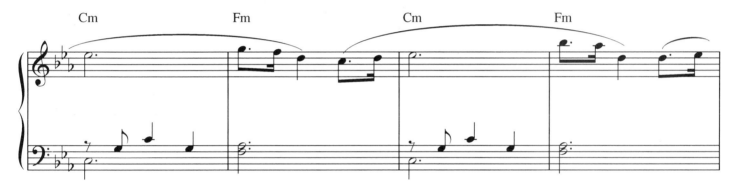

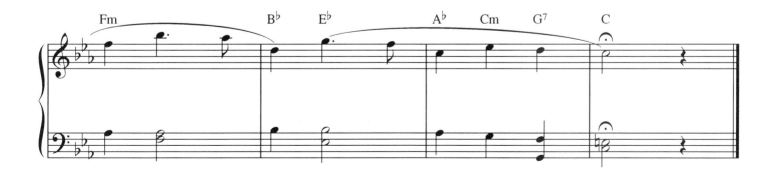

Lullaby

Music by Johannes Brahms

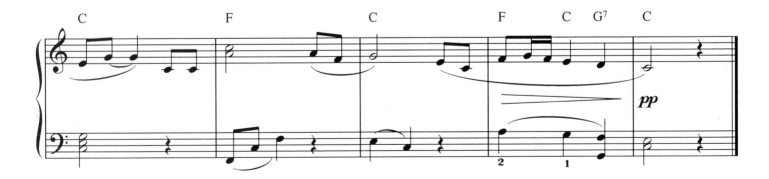

Prelude
Op. 28, No. 7

Music by Frédéric Chopin

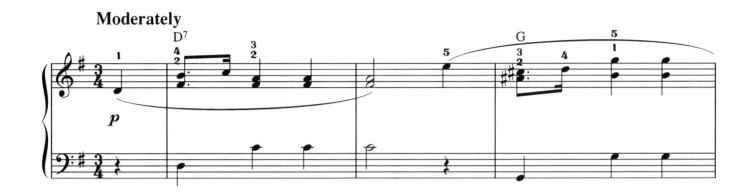

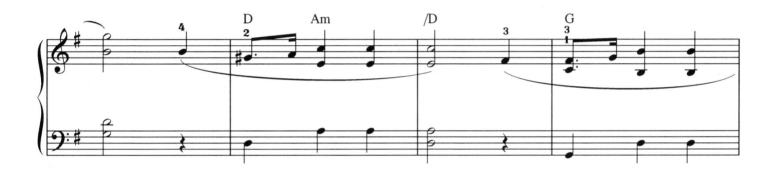

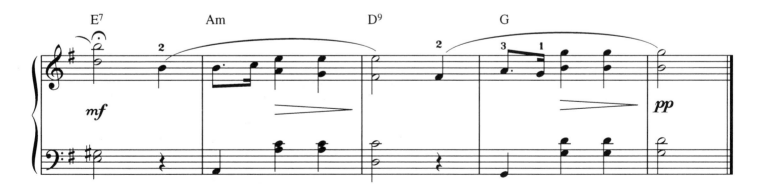

On Wings Of Song

Music by Felix Mendelssohn

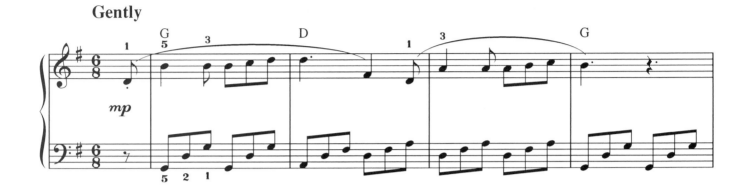

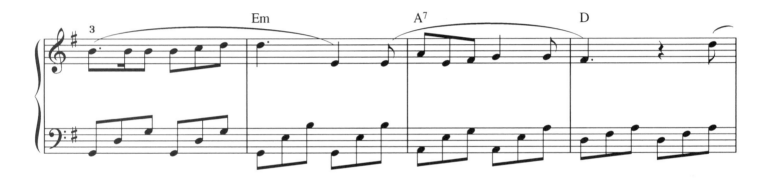

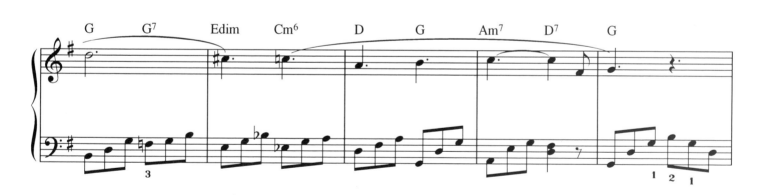

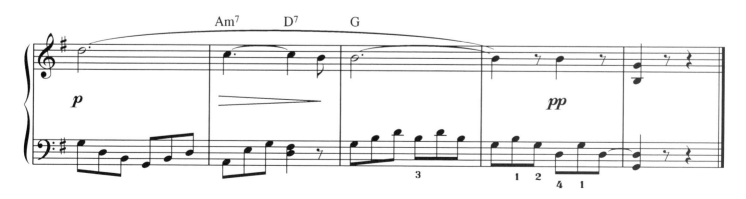

Pizzicato

From the ballet "Sylvia"

Music by Léo Delibes

With movement

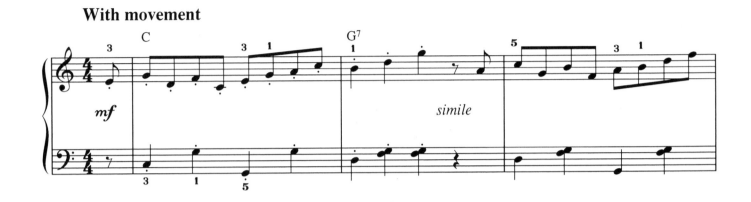

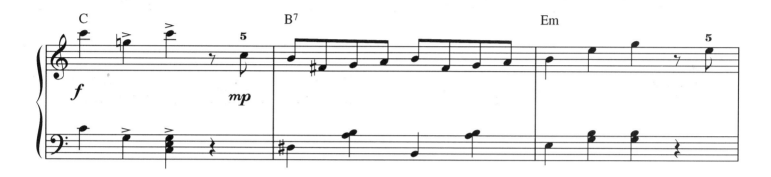

The Wild Horseman

From Album For The Young, Op.68

Music by Robert Schumann

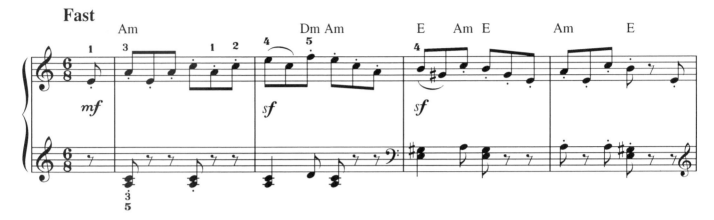

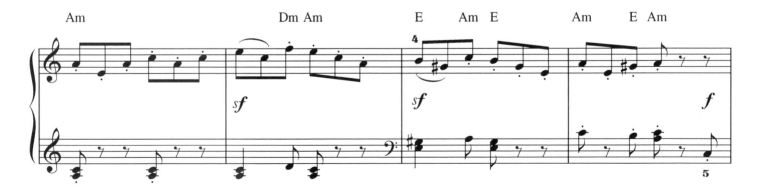

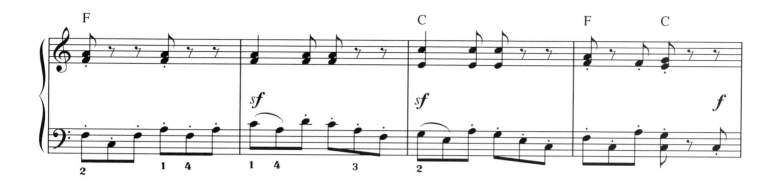

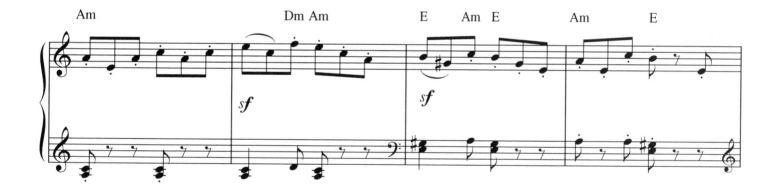

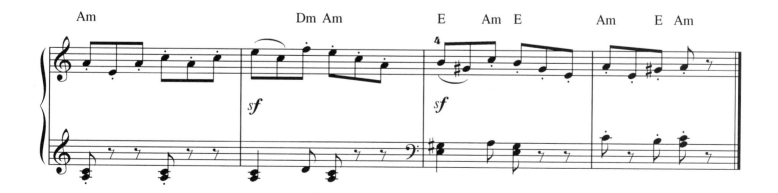

Panis Angelicus

Music by César Franck

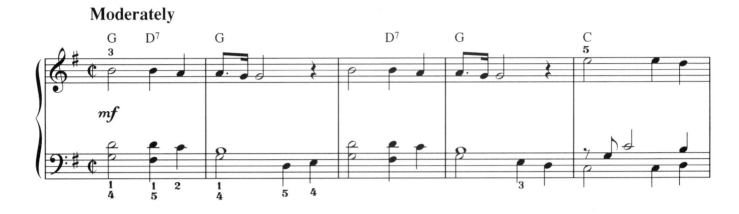

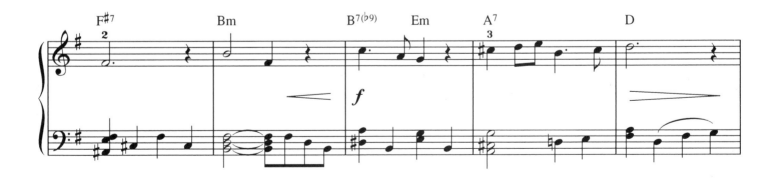

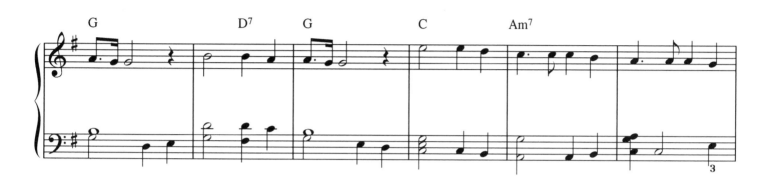

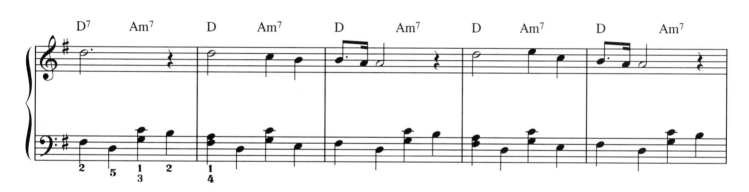

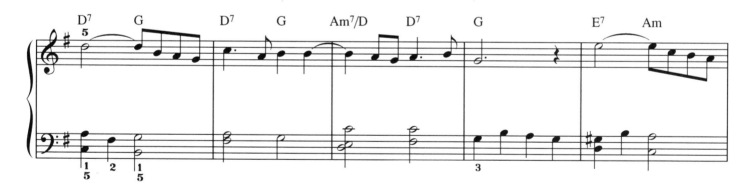

The Last Spring

Music by Edvard Grieg

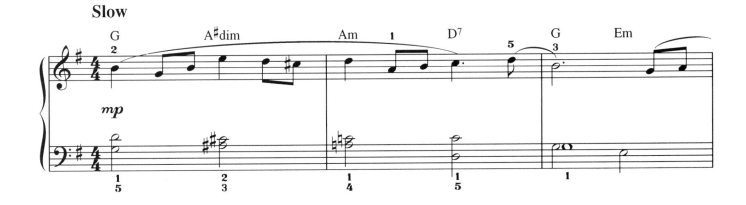

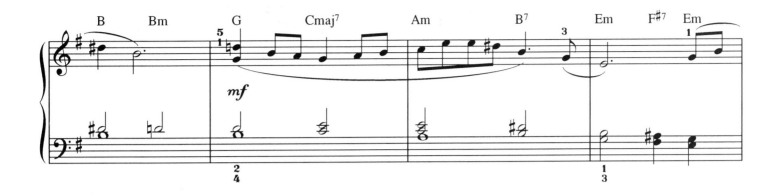

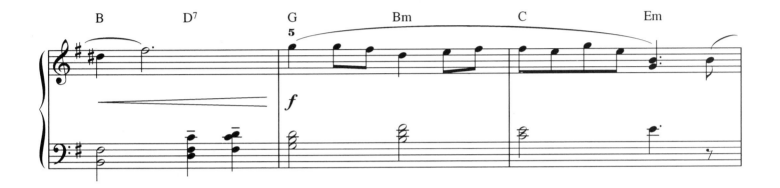

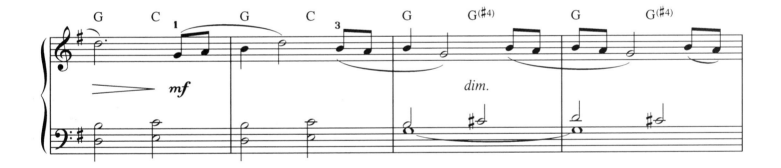

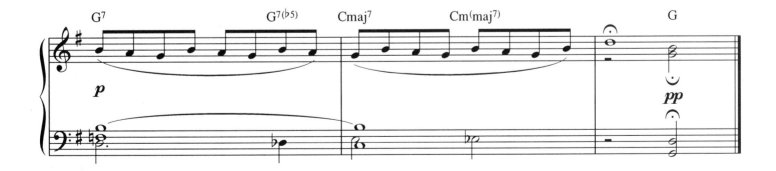

Waltz

From the ballet "Swan Lake"

Music by Pyotr Ilyich Tchaikovsky

Moderately

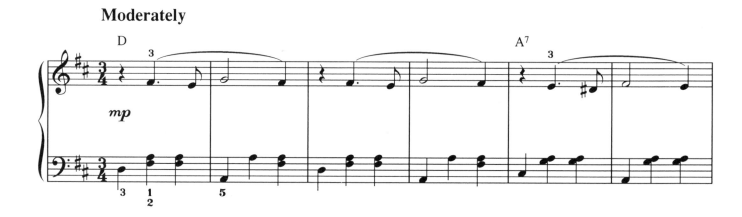

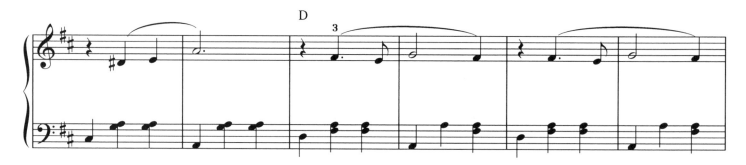

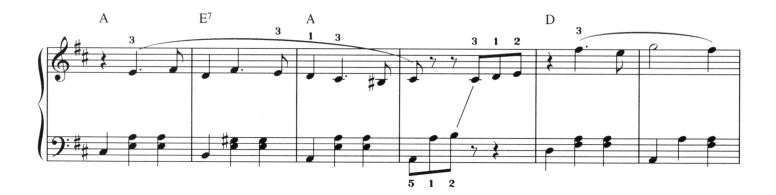

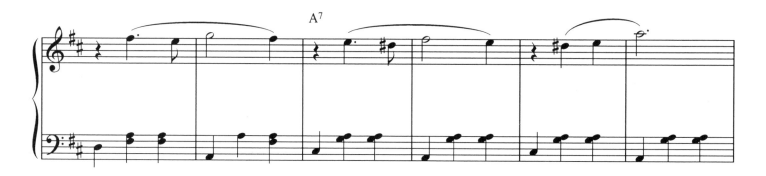

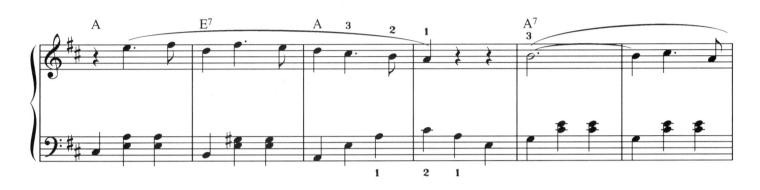

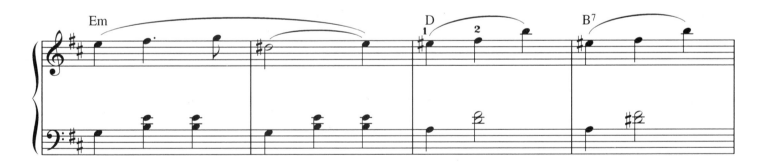

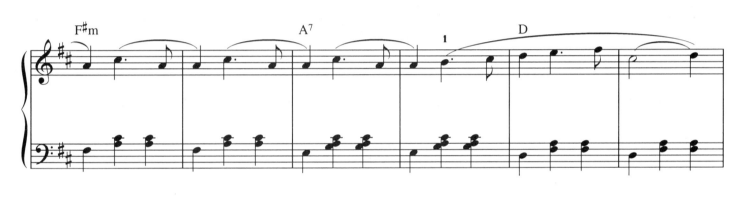

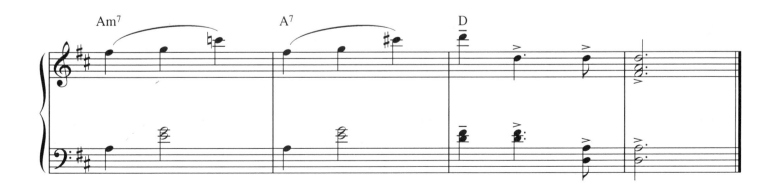

Chorus Of The Hebrew Slaves

From the opera "Nabucco"

Music by Giuseppe Verdi

Moderately

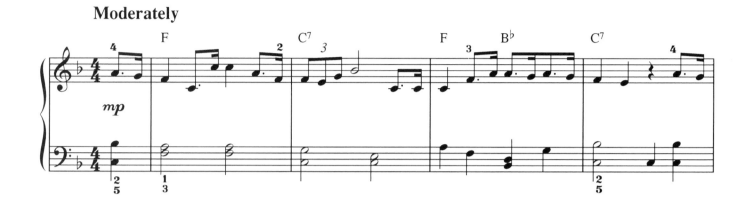

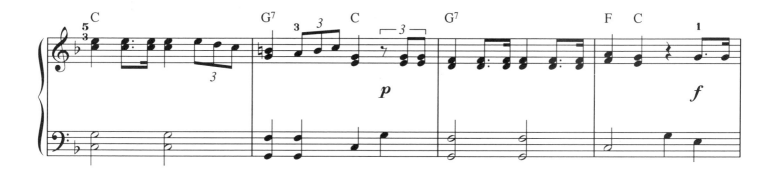

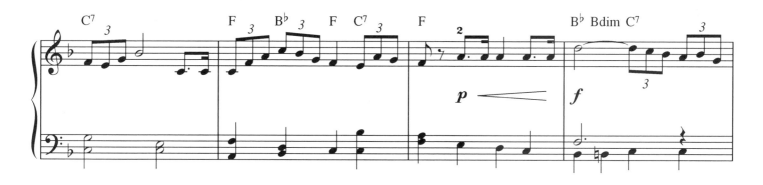

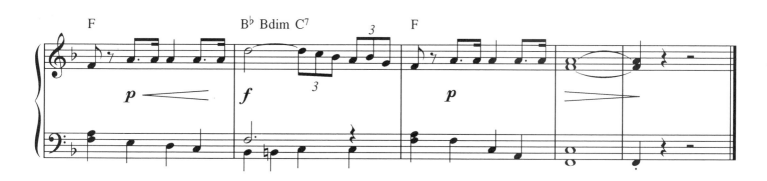

La Donna è Mobile

From the opera "Rigoletto"

Music by Giuseppe Verdi

Moderately

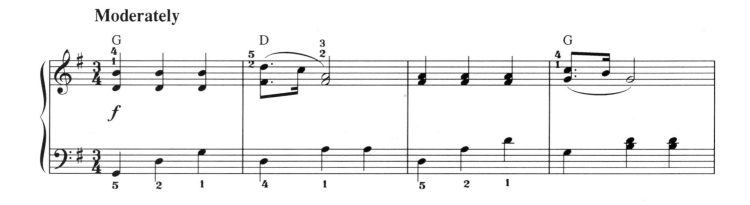

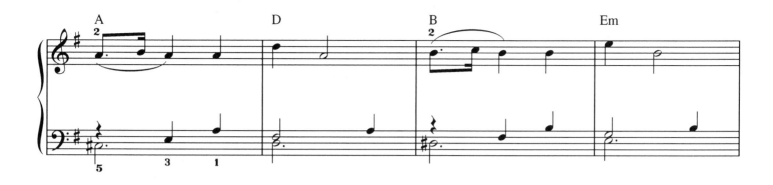

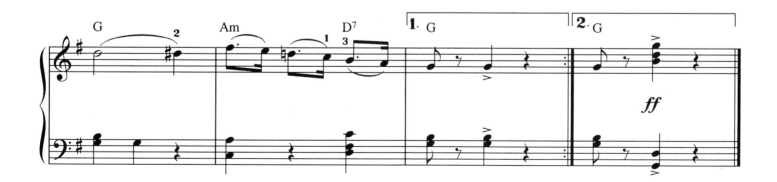

On With The Motley

From the opera "I Pagliacci"

Music by Ruggiero Leoncavallo

Slowly

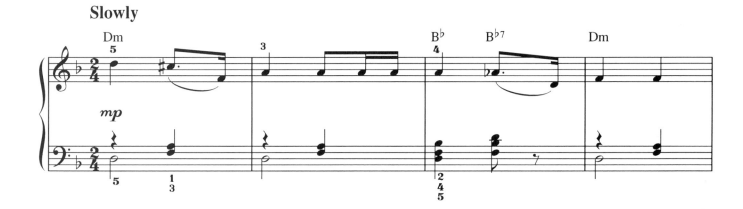

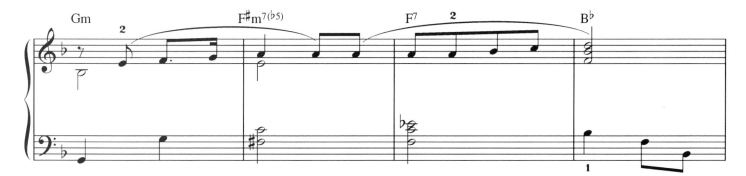

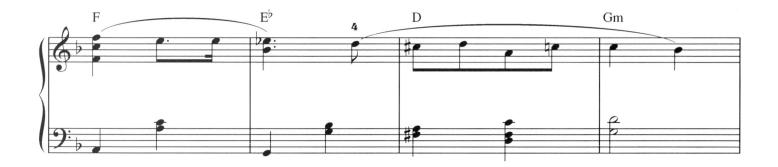

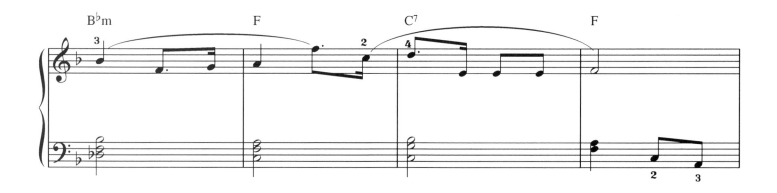

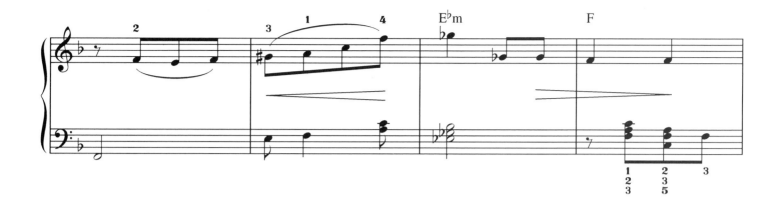

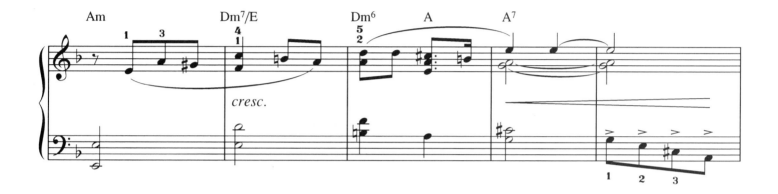

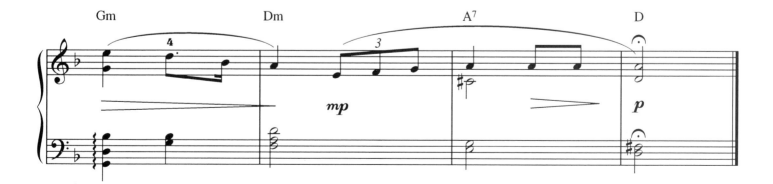

The Flower Song

From the opera "Carmen"

Music by Georges Bizet

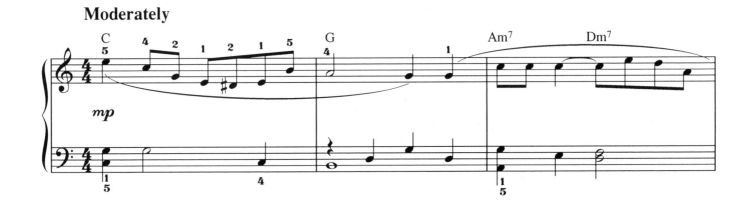

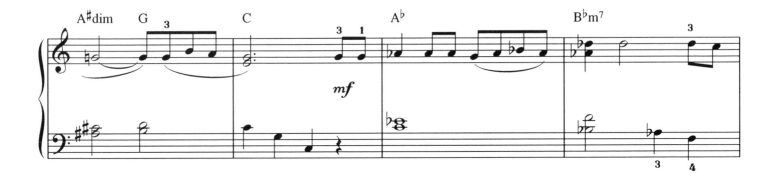

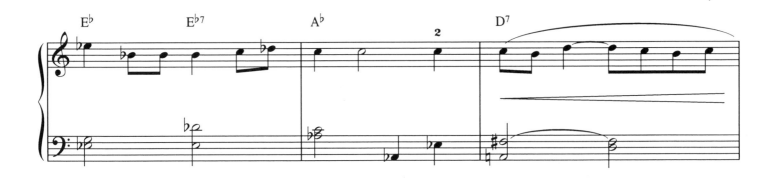

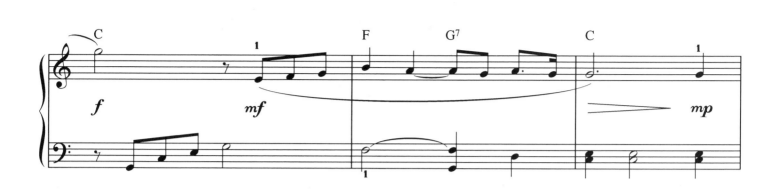

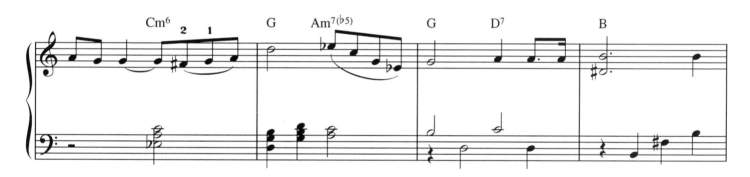

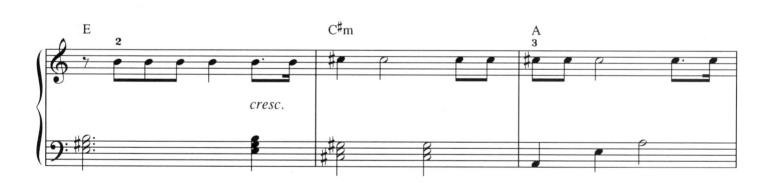

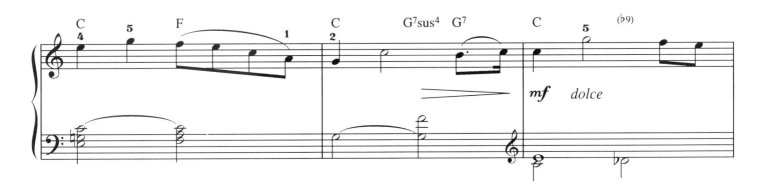

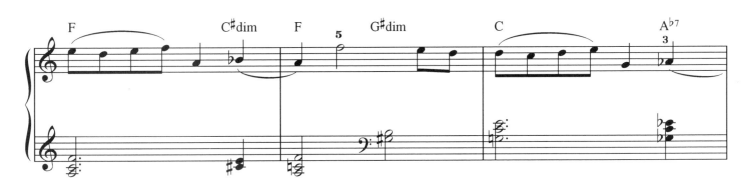

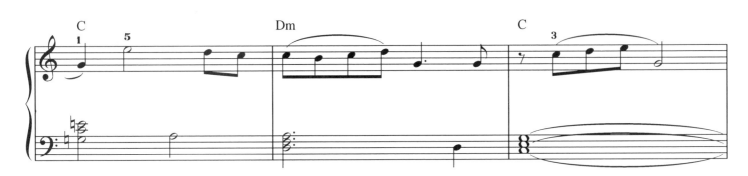

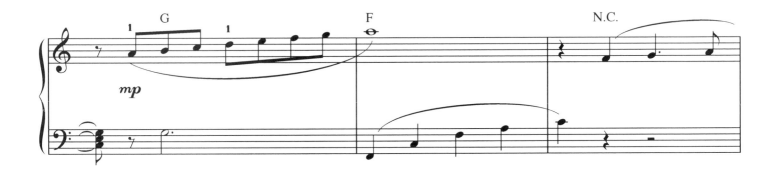

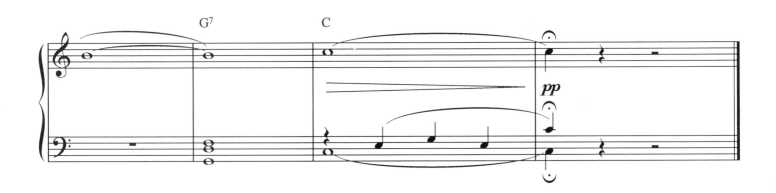